W9-BYJ-980

Adapting to the ENVIRONMENT

Text by Fulvio Cerfolli

Illustrations by Ivan Stalio

RSVP®

RAINTREE
STECK-VAUGHN
PUBLISHERS
A Steck-Vaughn Company

Austin, Texas

Published by Raintree Steck-Vaughn Publishers, an imprint
of Steck-Vaughn Company

Consultant: Gregory Haenel, Ph. D., Rutgers University
Editor: Kathy DeVico
Electronic Production: Lyda Guz, Scott Melcer
Project Manager: Joyce Spicer

Library of Congress Cataloging-in-Publication Data
Cerfolli, Fulvio.
      Adapting to the environment/text by Fulvio Cerfolli;
illustrated by Ivan Stalio.
           p.   cm — (Everyday life of animals)
      Includes bibliographical references and index.
      Summary: Describes how animals in different regions
adapt to their environment in order to survive, discussing
such habitats as deserts, freshwater wetlands, and the sea.
      ISBN 0-8172-4196-5
      1. Animals — Adaptation — Juvenile literature.
[1. Animals — Adaptation.   2. Habitat (Ecology)
3. Ecology.]   I. Stalio, Ivan, ill.   II. Title.   III. Series.
QL49.C45   1999
591.4 — dc21   97-51394
                                                          CIP
                                                          AC

Printed in Italy
Bound in the United States

1 2 3 4 5 6 7 8 9 0   02 01 00 99 98

Photo credits [and Acknowledgments] that appear on page 64
constitute an extension of this copyright page.

Contents

Introduction

Catta lemur

We are often amazed by an animal's appearance, by its behavior, or by its ability to survive in hostile surroundings. For example, the insect we know as the walkingstick escapes the attention of predators because it looks like a twig, and the great polar bear's white coat allows it to hunt unobserved in the snow-covered Arctic landscape. What surprises us most is that animals seem to be so perfectly adapted to the **environment** in which they live. The camel survives in deserts by drawing on reserves of water stored in many unique ways and by drawing on fat tissue stored in its hump; the tiny hummingbird sucks nectar from tropical flowers with its long beak and long sticky tongue, and its unique ability to hover in the air; and the fragile gazelle can survive in open grasslands, because its speed enables it to escape from **predators**.

Some animals, such as the golden eagle, live in small groups. Others, such as sardines, starlings, or locusts, move in huge numbers. Regardless of the size of the group, however, the individuals within it will all be different. Most wildebeests, for example, can keep ahead of cheetahs or lions (and are, we might say, well adapted for survival) while others, whether careless, old, or ill, will be caught.

Not only does a natural environment permit well-adapted individuals, but it also favors entire species if they are well suited to its special conditions. It is no accident that in the frozen ice and snow of the Arctic, polar bears, arctic foxes, hares, geese, baby seals, and grouse are all white, making it easy for them to blend in with their surroundings. In a given environment, any single species is just one of several life forms suited for survival there. Over the generations, animal species are transformed by **evolution**, some slowly and some quickly. Many will occupy new **territories**, take on new roles, and interact with new neighbors. To survive they have to adapt to continuous, unpredictable changes in their surroundings. For example, the long drought in the Galápagos Islands threatens Darwin's finch with extinction, while the clearing of forests in Madagascar is endangering the survival of lemurs.

Everywhere, whenever an animal is born, the game of life begins again. The newborn will have to survive accidents, sickness, and predators. If food or space is in short supply, it will have to compete with others. It will have to use the solutions its species provides it with or invent new ones. *Adapting to the Environment* introduces and explains some of the numerous ways that evolution has provided for animals to survive the continually changing conditions of the Earth.

Bald eagles (opposite)

Staying Alive

To ensure their survival, all animals, from huge blue whales and elephants to the tiny creatures that can only be seen through a microscope, must get enough food, defend themselves, rest, play, and produce young. They are all influenced daily by climate, the changing seasons, the alternation of day and night, and the cycles of the moon, among other things. Some environments are quite suitable for one type of animal and extremely unsuitable for another. For example, you are not likely to find a cheetah at the North Pole or a polar bear in Central Africa! The animals themselves influence and transform the **habitat** in which they live. Think of the way a huge herd of caribou will pack down the soil and vegetation, as thousands and thousands of animals pass along the same routes year after year. An animal's ability to survive in a given environment is greatly influenced by the amount of food available and by the number of predators or rivals in the area. Lack of food, overcrowding, scarcity of good sites for nests or dens, and predators are just some of the reasons that will cause a species to evolve, die out, or move on to a more suitable environment.

VICTORY TO THE SWIFT
Large predators, like cheetahs, need to be able to move faster than the animals on which they prey. Intelligence is important, too. Predators soon learn that young, old, or sick animals are slower and easier to catch than healthy adults.

A PROTECTIVE EYE
Butterfly fish have special elongated noses that are just right for pushing into cracks and crevices in rocks where food lies. But does sticking their nose into a rock leave their back undefended? No, because they have a large, black dot on their tail that fools predators into thinking it's an eye.

MEANT FOR FLIGHT
Birds have highly specialized adaptations for flight. These include strong wings, light bones, and an internal air-cooling system. The spoonbill also has a specially shaped beak that is ideal for finding and trapping its favorite foods—fish and aquatic insects.

NOW YOU SEE ME, NOW YOU DON'T
By imitating the color of the vegetation in its habitat, the Darwin's frog below protects itself from predators.

KEEPING SAFE
Puffins nest in huge clifftop **colonies**. Many larger seabirds can easily catch a small puffin in flight. To reduce the risk of being caught, puffins fly in groups when they leave the nest to get food.

Polar Regions

The dark polar winter is 6 months long. For the rest of the year, the sun never rises far above the horizon, and at the poles temperatures rarely rise above freezing. The Antarctic is colder than the Arctic. In the winter, temperatures at the poles can drop as low as –120° F (–84.4°C). Despite these harsh conditions, the polar regions are home to a host of animals. There is little vegetation, so the larger animals are mainly **carnivores**, feeding largely on the abundant fish in the oceans. Keeping warm is a top priority for **mammals** and birds. They have a number of **adaptations** to help them, including layers of fat under their skins and thick coats of fur or feathers. Some insects lie **dormant** under the snow during winter. Those who can't cope with the intense cold **migrate** south until spring.

GOOD FATHERS
Emperor penguins live in the Antarctic. During the coldest month of the year, each female lays a single egg. There is no nest. The male keeps the egg, and later the chick, on his feet, warmed by a fold of skin hanging from his belly. While the females return to the ocean to feed, the males **incubate** the eggs, without eating, for two long months. They huddle together in huge colonies for warmth, taking turns at being on the cold outer edges of the group. The females usually return with food just after the chicks hatch.

KILLER WHALES
These huge predators patrol the frigid coastlines in search of food. Killer whales hunt together in groups, forcing schools of fish into shallow waters before closing in for the kill or snapping up unsuspecting penguins or seals. To protect them from the cold, they have layers of insulating fat, called **blubber**.

THE WALRUS

Weighing in at about 2,600 pounds (1,180 kg), the male walrus is the largest land animal in the Arctic Circle. Besides humans, its only real enemy is the killer whale. It has a thick layer of blubber under its skin, which not only keeps it warm but also helps it to stay afloat (fat weighs less than the water). It also has two air pockets around its neck, which it puffs up and uses in the same way we use life jackets. The snout is covered with stiff but sensitive bristles, which a walrus uses to find shellfish, crabs, and sea urchins on the ocean floor. It scoops them up with its lips.

The walrus uses its long tusks like a can opener, to open oyster shells and **mollusks**. *It also uses its tusks to haul itself along the ice.*

A hungry polar bear will crouch for hours in the snow over a seal's breathing hole. It knows that sooner or later the seal will come up for air. When it does, the polar bear snatches it up with its paw at lightning speed.

THE GREAT WHITE HUNTER

Polar bears have thick, shaggy coats and a layer of fat under their skin to keep them warm. Their white or yellowish fur helps them blend into the snow-covered landscape. This makes them more successful hunters, since they can get close to their prey before being seen. Polar bears are good swimmers and divers, and their coats are also water-repellent. They have fur covering most of the soles of their feet as protection from the snow, while their long, curved claws help them grip the slippery **pack ice**, as well as prey. The female digs a den in a bank of snow, where she will give birth to her cubs. She keeps them in this warm home until spring.

■ **MORE ABOUT POLAR BEARS**

Polar bears live in the coastal regions around the North Pole. Adult bears can measure up to 11 feet (3.3 m) long from head to tail and 5 feet (1.5 m) tall at the shoulder. An adult male can weigh up to 1,800 pounds (810 kg). Polar bears like to travel and are often sighted perched on pieces of floating ice as they follow ocean **currents**, sometimes for hundreds of miles.

SEALS

The seal is the polar bear's favorite food (particularly the ringed seal). There are about eight species of seals in the Arctic Circle, and many more in other parts of the world. True seals are earless and well adapted to life in the water, although they flop along clumsily on land. They are excellent divers and can stay underwater for long periods of time. Seals feed largely on fish, crabs, and squid.

Tundra

The Arctic tundra is a vast rolling plain that runs across the far north of Scandinavia, Siberia, North America, and Greenland. The freezing climate produces a layer of **subsoil** that never thaws, called the **permafrost**. A top layer about 3 feet (1 m) thick thaws during the brief summer. At this time plants grow and animals reproduce quickly, while there is sufficient sunlight and warmth. Vegetation is patchy and low. There are no trees there because of the fierce winds. Only a few animal species live on the tundra all year long.

A COAT FOR ALL SEASONS
The arctic hare has a thick, white fur coat during the winter. This keeps it warm and helps it blend into the snowy landscape, making it hard for predators to spot. It also has thick fur on its paws, similar to winter gloves, so that they don't freeze as it hops around in the snow in search of food. When the snow melts in the spring and the landscape turns brown-gray, its coat changes to the same color as the surrounding countryside.

A LONG JOURNEY
The caribou is part of the deer family. It is closely related to the European reindeer. Caribou make the longest migratory journeys of any mammal. After wintering in the coniferous forests of Canada and Alaska, they head north to the tundra in the spring. They feed on the vegetation that flourishes there during the brief Arctic summer. Traveling in huge herds, they follow the same routes each year. Some travel up to 3,000 miles (4,800 km) round-trip.

A LIVING FORTRESS

Musk oxen are huge animals. Their only natural predators are wolves, which, hunting in packs, attack only old, sick, or very young animals. Adult musk oxen protect their young by standing together in a circle with their horns facing outward. The calves stay safe at the center of the circle.

■ MORE ABOUT MUSK OXEN

Musk oxen live in the Arctic coastal regions of Greenland and Canada. They have also been reintroduced into Alaska. Musk oxen have thick, shaggy coats reaching almost to their feet. Under the shaggy outer hair, there is a layer of wool that keeps them warm, even in freezing temperatures. They shed this inner layer during the summer, and some Arctic natives use it to weave fine cloth. As their name suggests, musk oxen have a strong, musky odor. Adult males, called bulls, stand about 5 feet (1.5 m) tall at the shoulder and weigh about 800 pounds (360 kg). Both males and females have long horns. Musk oxen feed on grass, **lichens**, and low-growing plants.

KEEPING THE REFRIGERATOR FULL

The arctic fox spends its whole life in the freezing tundra. Like the arctic hare, it changes the color of its coat according to the season. During the summer, when there is plenty of prey, it hunts continually. It catches far more than it can eat and buries its leftovers in the cold soil. The fox knows that this buried treasure will be good for months. Equipped with an excellent memory, the fox will find the spot during the winter, when food is scarce.

Coniferous Forests

The great northern forests extend across Siberia, Eastern Europe, Scandinavia, Canada, and Alaska, just south of the tundra. They form a ring around the top of the world about 7,500 miles (12,000 km) long. This area is also called the taiga or boreal forest. Most of the trees are **evergreen** conifers, including pines, spruces, and larches. The undergrowth is not very thick, and the forest floor is covered with moss, lichens, and grasses. Despite the cold climate, many animals make their homes in these forests.

SEARCHING FOR SEEDS

The crossbill gets its name from the shape of its beak, the upper part of which overlaps the lower to form a neat double hook. Crossbills feed exclusively on conifer seeds. Their beaks are special adaptations to help them pry seeds from the cones of coniferous trees. Crossbills leave the coniferous forest only when food is scarce. Then they fly long distances looking for a new home with enough food.

HOARDING FOR HARD TIMES AHEAD

Squirrels spend the summer and early fall gathering nuts, seeds, and mushrooms, among other things. They store them carefully away in the holes of trees or bury them underground. Some squirrels even dry the mushrooms before storing them so that they won't rot. The only problem with all this careful hoarding is that the squirrels appear to have bad memories and don't always remember where they have stored their food!

A SOLITARY FOREST DWELLER

The wolverine (known as the "glutton" in Europe) lives alone in the thickest part of the forest. It is active both day and night and is a fearless and cunning hunter. It will even attack wolves and bears as they return from the hunt to rob them of their kill. The wolverine resembles a small bear, but it has a long, bushy tail. It also has long, sharp claws and strong teeth.

Close-up of a crossbill, showing its peculiar overlapping beak. The shape of a bird's beak often indicates what kinds of food it eats.

RULER OF THE NIGHT

The horned owl lives in the woodlands of northern Europe and America. It is a **nocturnal** hunter with excellent night vision and good hearing. Horned owls feed mostly on mice and other small mammals.

A PRICKLY FOREST ANIMAL

The North American porcupine lives throughout the forests of Canada and the United States. It likes to eat green vegetation and the tender layer of tissue beneath the bark of trees. Sometimes it eats the bark around the bottom of a tree, thus killing it. Porcupines have long, stiff quills, which they display when threatened.

Broadleaf Forests

Broadleaf forests, also known as temperate or **deciduous** forests, consist largely of flowering trees with broad leaves. The leaves fall in the autumn, and new ones appear in the spring. Broadleaf forests occur mainly in the Northern Hemisphere, to the south of the coniferous forests. They grow where winters are not too cold and summers are not too hot, and where rain falls regularly. Temperate forests are much less extensive than they were in the past, because huge areas have been cleared for farming.

A VARIED DIET
The grizzly bear is an **omnivore**, which means it eats a little bit of everything, including grass, eggs, insects, roots, grubs, and honey. In North America, in the fall, when salmon return upstream to **spawn**, grizzlies love to go fishing.

MAKING TRACKS
Roe deer live in the broadleaf forests of Europe and Asia. During the winter, the bucks (males) live alone while the females and young stay together in small groups. As spring returns, the roe deer's winter coat changes from grayish brown to a brighter reddish brown color. During courtship, at the end of the summer, the male circles the female many times, often leaving circular or figure-eight tracks called **roe rings** in the undergrowth. The following spring, the doe gives birth to a single fawn. The fawns have spotted coats that help them blend in with their environment.

CHEMICAL WEAPONS
Skunks live in the forests of the Americas. Unlike other animals that have developed colorings that help them blend in to their environments, skunks have a conspicuous black-and-white coat. Being so visible is their way of warning predators to stay away. They have **glands** under their tail containing a foul-smelling liquid that they spray on attackers. The stench is so powerful that it can be sensed up to a mile away!

■ **MORE ABOUT HAWKS**
Hawks are birds of prey that live on every continent except Antarctica. The smaller ones are fast fliers and usually catch other birds in flight. The larger hawks, which include the European buzzard, feed mainly on prey that live on the ground. These hawks have long, broad wings on which they soar high in the sky, circling until they spot their prey. Then they swoop down to grab the animal. The male and female nest on high cliffs or in tall trees. The female lays three to four eggs and incubates them while her mate brings her food. They will defend their nesting site by threatening or attacking any intruders.

AMBUSH!
Many of the larger hawks fly quite slowly. For this reason they prefer to ambush their prey from the top of a tall rock or tree. They lie in wait until the chosen victim passes below, and then they dive downward. Some hawks especially like to eat vipers, although they are not immune to vipers' poison. Hawks can die after being bitten.

Grasslands

Grasslands cover huge areas of the Earth, usually places that are too dry for trees to grow. The African **savanna** and veld, the North American prairie, the South American pampas and llanos, the Australian bush, and the Asian steppes are all grasslands. As the name suggests, they are all covered with types of grass. They support vast numbers of insects, huge herds of **herbivores**, and some predators. Grazing animals, such as antelope and zebras, roam the African grasslands, while kangaroos bound about the Australian bush.

■ MORE ABOUT WILDEBEESTS

Wildebeests, also called gnu, are part of the antelope group. There are two species of wildebeests. The brindled gnu, or blue wildebeest, is the most common. The white-tailed variety has a dark brown coat and a white tail. It is now extinct in the wild and survives only in a few national parks and preserves. Most wildebeests are about 3 to 6 feet (1 to 1.7 m) tall at the shoulder. They are grazers, feeding on grass and low-growing shrubs. They often stay in groups with other animals, such as zebras or ostriches. Like all herbivores, wildebeests are always on guard against predators, especially the lion. Wildebeest calves are particularly vulnerable, and only the healthiest ones can survive.

A BUILT-IN AIR FILTER
Saigas live in herds on the steppes of Central Asia. Their strange, swollen-looking **muzzles** are a special adaptation to their environment. They use them to filter the freezing air in winter, warming it and also removing traces of dust before it reaches their lungs. Saigas have been hunted extensively for their horns, which are highly valued in Chinese medicine. The saiga is now a protected species.

THE BISON'S LAST STAND
Until recently, huge herds of North American buffalo grazed the prairies from Alberta, Canada, to New Mexico. As the weather grew warmer each spring, they moved north, giving birth to their young along the way. Sadly, the North American bison were almost wiped out last century by uncontrolled hunting. But protective laws enacted since then have allowed a few small populations to grow again. There is also a European bison. It is a very rare animal, protected in nature preserves and parks in Germany and Poland.

FLIGHTLESS BIRDS
Grasslands are home to the largest flightless birds in the world. The ostrich lives on the African savanna, the emu in the Australian bush, and the rhea (shown right) inhabits the pampas of South America. With the exception of humans, full-grown rheas have few enemies. However, chicks are vulnerable to attack by small mammals and birds of prey. For this reason, the eggs are incubated and the young safeguarded by their fathers, until the little ones are old enough to protect themselves.

HUGE HERDS ON THE MOVE
Wildebeests inhabit the vast savannas of central and eastern Africa. They live in large herds that are almost always on the move in search of new pastures. Each spring, mixed herds of wildebeests, zebras, and gazelles travel over 100 miles (160 km) from Kenya to the Serengeti Plain (in Serengeti National Park) in Tanzania. The animals make this difficult journey in order to reach richer pastures that will give their calves a better start in life.

Deserts

Deserts usually have very little permanent water, because the amount of rainfall is very low. Deserts of one kind or another cover about a third of the Earth's total land surface. Contrary to what many people think, a typical desert landscape does not consist of mile after mile of sand dunes. Usually they are rocky, barren, and mountainous. Some deserts, like the Sahara in Africa, are hot all year long. Others, such as the Gobi Desert in Asia, are cold in the winter. Hot deserts usually occur in subtropical zones, while cold-winter deserts are located at high altitudes, usually in the shadow of tall mountains that block rainfall. Life in the desert is tough, and only a few hardy plants and animals can survive. Insects, **reptiles**, some birds, and small mammals are the most common creatures. All desert-dwelling plants and animals have special adaptations to survive the extremes in temperature and long periods without water.

DESERT FOXES
The fennec fox is the same color as desert sand. It lives in the Sahara and Arabian deserts. It has two very large ears with exposed blood vessels, which help keep it cool in the heat. It has very keen hearing, which it uses to locate prey at a distance. The fennec fox is a nocturnal animal and a burrower. It spends the daytime resting in its cool den and comes out to hunt only at night.

■ MORE ABOUT CAMELS
There are two species of camels. One is the dromedary, or one-humped Arabian camel (shown right), used in Arabia and North Africa. The other, with two humps, is called the Bactrian camel. It lives in Central Asia. Both species have been **domesticated** and are used for riding and as pack animals. While some Bactrian camels still roam wild in the arid zones of Turkistan and Mongolia, virtually all Arabian camels are now domesticated. Only a few run wild in the Australian outback, where they were first introduced as domestic animals. In addition to being used for transportation, camels also are kept for their wool, milk, meat, and hides. Camels are gentle animals when handled properly, but they also can kick and bite when they are annoyed or treated badly.

SHIPS OF THE DESERT
A camel can survive in the desert for several weeks without food and for many days without drinking. It can go without food because it has a large store of fat in the hump on its back. It can survive without water for up to a week because it has many adaptations to slow down water absorption. These include a thick coat that restricts water loss, and highly efficient kidneys that process body wastes in urine with very low water content. When it finds water, it can drink up to 25 gallons (95 l) in just a few minutes.

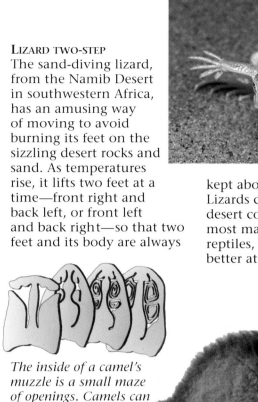

LIZARD TWO-STEP
The sand-diving lizard, from the Namib Desert in southwestern Africa, has an amusing way of moving to avoid burning its feet on the sizzling desert rocks and sand. As temperatures rise, it lifts two feet at a time—front right and back left, or front left and back right—so that two feet and its body are always kept above the hot ground. Lizards can survive parched desert conditions better than most mammals and other reptiles, because they are better at conserving water.

The inside of a camel's muzzle is a small maze of openings. Camels can close their nostrils and block out the sand.

A camel's large eyes are protected from the sand by long, thick eyelashes.

Camels kneel in the hot sand to rest. They have special pads to protect their chest, knees, and thigh joints from becoming burned.

Camels have two toes on each foot. These are joined by a web of skin that allows the foot to spread apart. This makes it easier for the camel to walk in the sand.

19

Tropical Rain Forests

Tropical rain forests grow in a narrow belt around the equator. There are almost no distinguishable seasons in this area. Temperatures remain at about 68–92°F (20–33°C) all year long, and it rains almost every day. Some places get well over 150 inches (380 cm) of rain every year. The rain forest has several layers, or strata. The highest layer contains the tops of the tallest trees, called **emergents**. The second layer is the thick **canopy**. It is formed by trees whose crowns touch, blocking the sunlight from the lower levels. Below the canopy is a layer of shrubs and young trees, and then there is the forest floor. Not many plants grow on the forest floor because it is so dark. Even though they cover less than one-fifth of the Earth's land surface, rain forests contain over half the known plant and animal species.

FOREST-FLOOR GARDENERS

Leaf-cutting ants live in huge underground colonies in the forests of Central and South America. Each colony grows its own food in the form of **microscopic** mushrooms, or fungi. The ants scour the forest for suitable leaves, which they cut off and carry back to their nests. Other ants chew the leaves and put them into special "gardens" where the fungus grows on them. The ants tend these "gardens" and harvest the mushrooms when they are ready.

A SACRED BIRD

The quetzal is a very rare bird. It lives in the depths of the tropical rain forests of Central America. It was considered sacred by the ancient Aztec and Mayan people. The male is about the same size as a pigeon. It has bright green tail feathers that can grow to over 3 feet (1 m) in length. Many rain forest birds are brightly colored. This helps them blend in with the bright flowers and fruits of the tropical forest. The male quetzal is probably the most brightly colored of them all.

Gibbons are tree-dwelling apes that live in the rain forests of Southeast Asia. There are about nine species of gibbons. They are all quite small in size. The largest species, called the siamang, grows to about 3 feet (1 m) in length. Most of the others are about 20 inches (50 cm) long. Gibbons are omnivores and feed on fruit, shoots, small mammals, birds' eggs, insects, and some **invertebrates**. Although they usually stay in the trees, gibbons walk in an upright position with their arms held up in front or behind them when they are on the ground. They live in small family groups, and each group defends a territory of about 50 acres (20 ha). They warn other gibbons to keep out by emitting loud calls.

JUNGLE ACROBATS
Gibbons spend almost all their lives in the trees. Perfectly adapted for moving rapidly through the thick forest canopy, they have very mobile shoulder joints, long fingers and toes for gripping branches, and very long arms. They can move effortlessly through the trees, hand over hand, from branch to branch.

A DEADLY HUNTER
The green anaconda is one of the longest snakes in the world. It lives along the tropical rivers in South America. It usually is dark green with large, black spots. It hunts along the rivers by lying in wait until animals come to drink. It kills by squeezing its victim with its long, coiling body.

Mountains

Going up a mountain is a bit like making a journey toward the poles. Temperatures drop about 1.1°F (.6°C) every 300 feet (90 m), and vegetation changes accordingly. A typical mountain might have broadleaf forests at lower altitudes, followed by coniferous forests, then alpine grass and scrub, and, near the peaks, bare gravel and ice. Animals that live in the mountains must be able to tolerate freezing temperatures, high winds, and intense sunlight. Many migrate up the mountain in the spring and down to the warmer valleys in the winter. Others have adaptations that allow them to stay on the mountain all year. Some insects, such as springtails, can survive frozen in ice for up to 3 years.

ATHLETIC GOATS
Alpine ibex are at home among cliffs and crags high in the mountains, near the **snow line**. At this altitude they are safe from most predators, such as wolves. Their special split hooves with soft outer edges help them grip onto sheer rock. Within just a few days of birth, young ibex can follow their mothers along narrow cliff ledges and leap with them down steep mountainsides.

MOUNTAIN LIONS
The cougar, also called puma or mountain lion, is one of the largest cats in the Americas. It ranges from British Columbia to South America. Cougars can survive in very different habitats, from sea level forests and swamps to mountain peaks up to 15,000 feet (4,572 m). Excessive hunting has drastically reduced their numbers in North America, and they now live mainly in wilderness areas in and around the Rocky Mountains and the Andes. Cougars live alone. Each cat marks a large territory of up to 154 square miles (400 sq km) and defends it from others of its species.

HIGHLAND GRAZERS
Yaks are a large, massively built species of cattle. They live at very high altitudes about 14,000 feet (4,260 m) on the plateaus and mountains of Tibet and nearby regions. Their thick, wool coats protect them from the freezing cold. Yaks graze on grass and need a lot of water. They are said to eat snow in the winter. Wild yaks have been hunted to the point of near **extinction**. Domestic yaks are used for milk, butter, meat, and leather.

High fliers

The golden eagle is a large bird of prey with a wingspread of nearly 7 feet (2.1 m). It lives in the mountain forests and open grasslands of North America, Asia, and Europe. Golden eagles make their nests, called aeries, high on tall cliffs or lone trees. They are superb fliers and can glide for hours on mountain air currents. With their keen eyesight, they can spot prey far in the distance. The golden eagle is the national bird of Mexico.

Tropical mountain dwellers

When mountains are close to the equator, climate and vegetation are different. Below the alpine scrub and grass, the lower slopes are covered with thick bamboo forests. The mountain gorilla is one of the largest mammals to inhabit a tropical mountain forest. It lives near the equator in western and central Africa. Mountain gorillas are officially listed as an **endangered species**. In the case of one form, there are only about 500 to 1,000 individuals left in the wild. They are threatened with extinction because their forests have been cleared for farmland, and because they are hunted for gorilla "trophies" made from their heads, hands, and skins.

Freshwater Wetlands

Freshwater wetlands are found throughout the world, in a wide range of climates. They are generally divided into still (lake, pond, swamp) and flowing (river, stream) environments. They include everything from a temporary mud puddle to the Great Lakes, and from a small brook to the mighty Amazon River. Wetlands are constantly changing; lakes build up silt over time and can turn into swamps or marshland. Rivers often change their courses. Even so, most of these environments host large and varied communities of animals and plants, all of which are adapted to life in or around freshwater. Wetlands are fragile environments and have suffered greatly from pollution.

DRIP-DRY COAT
The variety of water shrew that lives around the edges of ponds in northern Europe and Asia has long, hair-fringed toes and is an excellent swimmer. Its thick pelt is water-resistant, so that it drips dry as soon as it emerges from the water. Water shrews hunt at night, feeding on small aquatic animals. They are courageous hunters and will attack prey much larger than themselves.

ENORMOUS REPTILES
There are two species of alligators. The lesser-known Chinese alligator lives along the Yangtze River. The American alligator lives in the south-eastern United States, where it lives in swamps and streams and lies in wait for prey such as fish, small mammals, and birds. Alligators have powerful tails that they use for defense and swimming. They dig burrows in which they rest and **hibernate** in cold weather.

LURKING PREDATORS

Northern pike lie perfectly still among the weeds around the edges of lakes and streams. When an unsuspecting fish or insect passes by, they lunge and attack viciously. Pike play an important role in limiting the number of fast-breeding fish that might otherwise become too abundant in small environments. Pike grow quite large and can weigh up to 35 pounds (16 kg).

THE WATER SPIDER

Unique among its fellow air-breathing spiders, the water spider spends most of its life underwater. It spins a silk web anchored to plants on the bottom of shallow lakes and ponds. It then fills the web with air bubbles that it carries down from the surface. When its underwater home is complete, the water spider carries out all its activities there.

WALKING ON WATER

Jacanas are waterbirds with extremely long toes and claws, which allow them to walk on floating vegetation, such as the leaves of water lilies (for this reason they are often called "lily-trotters"). They live in marshlands, rice fields, and ponds in tropical areas of the world. As they walk nimbly from leaf to leaf, they feed on insects, mollusks, small fish, and the seeds of aquatic plants.

Coastal Environments

The seashore is a narrow habitat between the land and the ocean. It stretches from the "splash zone," where only the biggest waves wet the shore at high tide, right down to the level of the lowest low tide. Biologists divide the shore into several zones. The upper zones are exposed to the air for much longer than the lower parts of the shore, so each zone supports different kinds of plants and animals. The regular movements of the tide and the breaking of the waves make life difficult. Many plants and animals have adaptations allowing them to cling tightly to rocks so that they are not swept out to sea. Many animals also have hard shells that protect them from the crashing waves.

SCARLET FEATHERS
The beautiful scarlet ibis lives in many wetland habitats along the coasts of northern South America. It has a long, downward-curving bill used to poke into the muddy shoreline and under mangrove roots to draw out the fish, insects, and frogs on which it feeds. Up until just a few years ago, the scarlet ibis nested in trees in huge colonies all along the coast. But because of overhunting, it is now an endangered species.

ROCK POOLS
The tide goes in and out roughly twice each day. As the ocean retreats over rocky areas, a certain amount of water is trapped in the cavities between rocks. Each of these rock pools hosts an entire community of animals and plants. Seagulls inspect the pools often to see if any fish have been trapped.

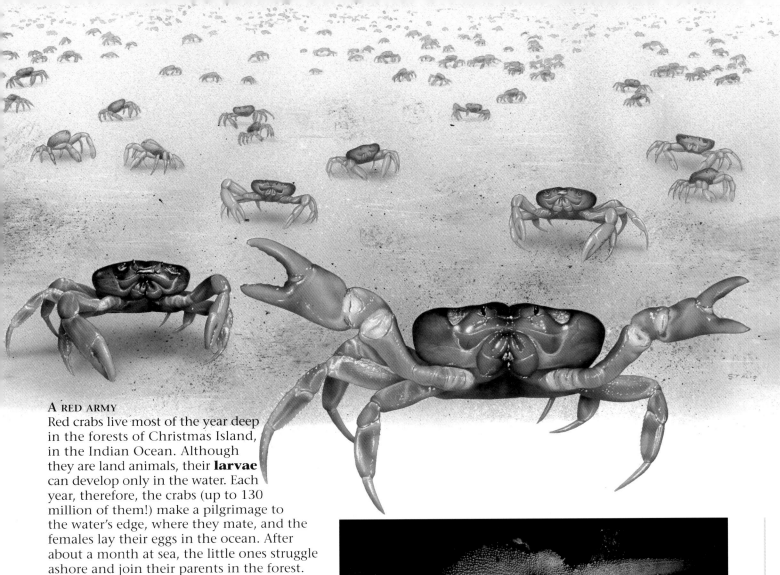

A RED ARMY

Red crabs live most of the year deep in the forests of Christmas Island, in the Indian Ocean. Although they are land animals, their **larvae** can develop only in the water. Each year, therefore, the crabs (up to 130 million of them!) make a pilgrimage to the water's edge, where they mate, and the females lay their eggs in the ocean. After about a month at sea, the little ones struggle ashore and join their parents in the forest.

EIGHT-ARMED PREDATORS

The octopus lives in rocky crevices in shallow water. It has two rows of suckers along the underside of each tentacle, which it uses to cling to the rocks and to move along. It eats crabs and other crustaceans. It can change its skin color according to its mood. It also shoots a cloud of "ink" at predators and escapes while its attacker is confused.

A GLEAMING SHELL

Cowries are sea snails that live in the Indian and Pacific oceans. Many of them have beautifully colored, glossy shells. They come out at night to hunt for food. One Mediterranean cowrie, called *Luria lurida*, resembles a sponge in color and deceives the octopus, which is its main predator.

Marine Environments

The seas and oceans form a huge environment and cover almost three-quarters of the Earth's surface. Life on our planet began in the ocean, and even today every part of it is inhabited. Seawater is an excellent place for life. It contains lots of oxygen plus many other life-sustaining elements. The ocean **food chain** is based on tiny plants and animals called **plankton** that drift in the surface waters. The highest density of life is found in the warmer, sunlit, upper 300 feet (90 m). But even the dark ocean depths thousands of feet below the surface are inhabited by worms, mollusks, fish, and other unique creatures.

SKILLED SWIMMERS
Dolphins have streamlined, torpedo-shaped bodies that are perfectly adapted to life in the water. Dolphins are superb and rapid swimmers. As they skim along underwater, their skin shifts in folds and ripples in response to water pressure. Body heat is maintained by a layer of blubber under the skin.

■ MORE ABOUT DOLPHINS
Despite their fishlike appearance, dolphins are mammals. They are warm-blooded with a stable body temperature. They breathe air with their lungs, and they give birth to live young, which feed on milk. They belong to a group of oceangoing mammals that also includes whales and porpoises. There are more than 50 species of dolphins. Most live in oceans in various parts of the world, but about a dozen species live in freshwater rivers in South America and Asia. Dolphins are intelligent, and most are friendly. They have been known to save people from drowning and ward off shark attacks. Dolphins emit a steady stream of **ultrasonic** sounds (clicks, whistles, etc.) as they move through the water. These sounds bounce off objects in their path, helping them build a mental picture of their surroundings.

WINGED WANDERER OF THE OCEANS
Albatrosses spend almost all their life at sea. They only come ashore to reproduce. Albatrosses are spectacular gliding birds and can "ride" ocean wind currents for hours without flapping their wings. They live mainly in the windswept ocean belt lying between Antarctica and the southernmost parts of Australia, South America, and Africa. They feed on plankton, fish, squid, and crustaceans, which they pick up on the ocean surface or just beneath the waves. They also follow fishing boats and **scavenge** the offal (waste fish) thrown overboard.

A SEA GIANT
The leatherback is the largest sea turtle in the world. It can weigh up to 1,600 pounds (725 kg) and measure up to 7 feet (2.1 m) in length. Leatherbacks spend all their lives at sea, coming ashore only to lay their eggs on tropical and subtropical beaches. The females crawl up the beach at night, until they are above the high tide line. They dig a hole with their flippers and deposit hundreds of eggs. The eggs hatch after about 7 to 10 weeks. Hatchlings scramble toward the ocean, but some are eaten by seabirds before they even reach the water.

THE LARGEST FISH IN THE WORLD
The whale shark is the largest known fish in the world. The longest whale shark ever measured was 50 feet (15 m) long, although there have been reports of much larger specimens. The whale shark is a rare animal and lives mainly in warm tropical seas where it swims lazily along the surface with its mouth open. A member of the shark order, the whale shark has only tiny teeth and feeds on the tiny planktonic creatures that float in the water. It is not aggressive and normally won't even try to defend itself if attacked.

Islands

Islands, surrounded by huge expanses of sea or ocean, are among the most isolated habitats in the world. Because they often are distant and hard to reach, they usually have fewer species of plants and animals than mainland environments. New islands are normally colonized by animals that arrive by accident, carried by wind or ocean currents. But when new creatures arrive on an island, not all of them are able to adapt to the special environment there. When island-dwelling creatures live in isolation for long periods of time, they often evolve in completely different ways from mainland species of the same group. For example, a common evolutionary change in many island birds and insects is that, although they still have wings, they can no longer fly.

A LONG SEA JOURNEY
Drifting on an ocean current is one of the most common ways that animals reach an island. Some biologists think the marine iguana of the Galápagos Islands came from South America in this way. The marine iguanas are the only group of iguanas adapted for life in saltwater. They have a rounded snout, slightly webbed feet, and a compressed tail to help them swim. They feed on seaweed growing in the shallow coastal waters.

THE HEAVIEST PARROT IN THE WORLD
Many island birds lose the ability to fly. The kakapo, a parrot native to New Zealand, is one of the rarest examples of flightless island birds. Before the Maori people arrived in New Zealand about 1,000 years ago, there were no large predators, and the country was a paradise for birds, many of which were flightless. The kakapo is the only parrot in the world that can't fly. It also is the heaviest, weighing up to 8 pounds (3.6 kg).

SEPARATE DEVELOPMENT
Lemurs are unique to the tropical forests of Madagascar and its adjacent islands, off the southern coast of Africa. They are relatives of monkeys and apes; biologists believe they have common ancestry. Sometime during the middle of the **Jurassic Period**, about 180 million years ago, the huge island of Madagascar detached itself from mainland Africa and began drifting eastward. From that time on, the animals on the island evolved separately from the ones on the mainland. In Africa, modern apes and monkeys developed, while the lemurs evolved on Madagascar.

■ **MORE ABOUT KAKAPOS**
Kakapos survive on two tiny islands near southern New Zealand (Little Barrier and Codfish). They are a highly endangered species, and just a few specimens are known to be still alive. Despite hard work by naturalists, it seems unlikely that the kakapos will make it far into the 21st century. They nest on the ground and are very vulnerable to predators, including cats, rats, and ermines. Even when they are shifted to isolated islands, predators always seem to arrive, making short work of the populations carefully introduced by scientists. Kakapos have an unusual mating ritual. The male digs a "bowl" in an open space in the forest. Then he sits in it and makes loud "booming" noises like a foghorn to attract females. If a female comes, the pair perform a strange dance before mating.

Domestic Animals

Over the centuries, humans have tamed a wide variety of animals that can be useful to them. The main uses include providing milk, meat, eggs, wool, entertainment, and company. The first attempts to domesticate animals were made over 10,000 years ago. Dogs were probably the first animals to live alongside humans, as they helped early hunters capture wild animals. Goats and sheep also were among the first animals to be domesticated by early farmers. Domesticated animals often bear little resemblance to their wild relatives, because people try to breed special characteristics into the animals they select.

FROM COCKFIGHTERS TO EGG LAYERS
The first domestic chickens were probably kept for entertainment as cockfighters. Later they came to have religious significance. The ancient Greeks used them in religious sacrifices. Keeping hens for their eggs is a recent development. Wild hens lay only about 10 eggs each year. Domestic hens lay over 200 eggs a year.

OUR NOBLEST FRIEND
The Asian wild horse, also called Przewalski's horse, is one of the three types of wild horses that gave rise to modern domesticated breeds. Although horses were among the last animals to be tamed, their domestication changed human lives considerably. Early humans hunted wild horses for meat and skins. Then, about 3,000 to 4,000 years ago, horses began to be used for transportation. The taming of horses was important in the founding and extension of modern civilization. Only recently, with the development of mechanized transportation, has the horse been replaced.

HELPFUL SHEEP

There are many varieties of sheep. Some are suited to life in hot desert climates, such as those in the Middle East. Others thrive in the cool climates of northern Scotland or southern New Zealand. Sheep are kept for their meat, wool, and milk. They were first tamed about 7,000 years ago in the Middle East. They feed on grass and low-growing herbs, which they then **regurgitate** and chew. This enables their four separate stomach compartments to digest them thoroughly.

DOMESTIC HUNTERS

The cat was considered a sacred animal in ancient Egypt about 5,000 years ago. They were domesticated there at least 3,500 years ago. The Egyptians probably tamed the cat when they realized it could protect their granaries (storehouses for grains) from mice and other **rodents**. The practice of keeping domestic cats quickly spread throughout the world. Domestic cats are smaller than most of their wild relatives (e.g. lions or tigers). Although cats have become thoroughly tamed, instinct dies hard, and many domestic cats are keen hunters. This cat, for example, seems to be considering catching another common domestic animal, the goldfish.

OUR BEST FRIEND

The association between dogs and humans began many thousands of years ago, probably when dogs began to take part in hunting expeditions or took to hanging around human encampments looking for leftover food. It is thought that humans came to rely on their dogs' barking to warn them of approaching danger. Over the centuries **selective breeding** by humans has produced an enormous variety of dogs, ranging from the tiny Chihuahua to the huge Saint Bernard and the Great Dane.

Life in the Dark

Many animals spend much, or even all, of their lives below the Earth's surface. They live in caves, underground streams and lakes, and in the soil beneath our feet. Surviving underground requires some highly specialized adaptations, including strong limbs or other features for tunneling. The animals also need a good sense of smell or touch for finding food, because there is no light for them to see by. Many underground animals are blind, and some have no eyes at all. Worms and many other animals feed on plant roots or on dead and decaying matter in the soil. Moles feed mainly on worms.

PINK, WRINKLED, AND BALD Naked mole rats, also called sand puppies, live in burrows under the African savanna. Up to one hundred of these mouse-sized creatures live in each burrow. Although they are blind, their eyes are sensitive to air currents, so they can tell when the tunnels are damaged and repair them.

COMING UP FOR AIR Moles spend most of their lives in burrows underground. They have long, strong claws for digging. A mole burrow can be up to 600 feet (180 m) long, although the norm is a bit shorter. Such extensive tunnel systems need good ventilation. To achieve this, as the moles dig they break the surface every now and then, leaving a hole where air can enter and blow through the burrow. The little piles of earth on the surface, called molehills, are signs of these ventilation holes.

SLEEPING UPSIDE-DOWN
Many species of bats roost in caves or crevices, where they hang upside-down by their feet. Sometimes thousands of bats roost together in a single cave.

RECYCLING WASTE MATERIAL
Bats produce a lot of waste material. Some animals, such as blind beetles and white and transparent invertebrates, feed on this. Called *guano*, it is mined and used as an agricultural fertilizer in many parts of the world.

A PINK CAVE DRAGON
The olm spends all its life in complete darkness in underground streams and pools. Although it has eyes when it is born, these organs are never used and gradually disappear. Olms are a pale pink color with bright red gills. They grow to about 12 inches (30 cm) long. They are becoming increasingly rare as pollution destroys their natural habitat.

Defense

With the exception of a few of the larger predators, all animals are on the lookout for other predators. One slip or unguarded moment could cost them their lives. For this reason, many species have developed special weapons to defend themselves against attacks. These include stingers, spines, quills, claws, and nippers. Other animals have learned to stay together in schools, swarms, or flocks, moving together like an army. This often makes them seem like a single large body, confusing and frightening potential predators. Some herd animals use chemical weapons, such as a strong-smelling scent, to warn the rest of the herd of danger.

SAFETY IN NUMBERS
Thousands of starlings swirling together in a huge flock are a menacing sight for potential attackers. Predators may be fooled into thinking they are looking at a single large animal. They also may be confused by the numbers and not know which bird to attack.

THE PERFECT WEAPON
Although there are over 1,500 species of scorpions, they all have the same basic body structure. They have eight legs, plus two large pincers at the front of their long bodies. These are used for grasping prey and tearing it apart. Scorpions also have a dangerous tail sting. They use this both to hunt and to protect themselves from predators.

A BALL OF SPINES
Most Europeans are familiar with the sociable hedgehog that lives in woods, gardens, and parks throughout the continent. The hedgehog is a friendly animal but has a fearful weapon when danger threatens. Its back and sides are covered with thousands of long, pointed spines. When it feels threatened, it erects the spines while curling itself into a tight ball. With its soft, furry stomach well hidden, it is perfectly safe. Any predators that dare to come too close get badly pricked.

BOUNDING LEAPS AS WARNING SIGNS

Impalas stay together in herds, their sensitive ears pricked for sounds of approaching predators. When attacked, there is little they can do but run away. However, as they escape, they make a great startling leap while releasing a strong scent from glands in their hindquarters. Both are warning signals for the rest of the herd.

A BIG APPEARANCE

This young, long-eared owl has already learned that when faced with danger it can puff up its feathers to make itself look larger and scarier than it actually is. This may be sufficient to frighten away a predator.

STAYING IN SCHOOLS

Many fish, particularly the smaller varieties, swim together in groups called schools. Like the starlings shown on the previous page, they move as a group to confuse predators, who don't know which individual to attack. Some very compact schools may also look like a large single animal to predators.

Homes

A home can be more than just shelter from the natural elements, such as heat, cold, wind, and rain. A good den, nest, or shell can protect against predators, be used as a storehouse for extra food, or a nursery for giving birth and bringing up young. In the grasslands of North America, where trees are rare and provide little shelter, rodents called prairie dogs build their homes underground. They live in colonies, sometimes made up of thousands of individuals, and their burrows are like cities.

A young prairie dog seeks reassurance from a watchful parent.

LIFE UNDERGROUND
Prairie dogs spend most of their lives underground. They dig huge networks of interconnecting tunnels down to about 12 feet (3.6 m) in depth. The dens, on various levels, are used for resting, raising the family, or as hideaways from predators. The dogs leave the burrow mostly to search for food. Once outside they keep a close lookout for rattlesnakes, ferrets, owls, and eagles. At the least sign of danger, they race back to the safety of their underground homes. Sometimes rattlesnakes or owls live in abandoned prairie dog burrows.

Exit holes are located at the tops of little mounds, from which the prairie dog can keep a lookout. The cone shape of the mounds also prevents flooding and lets in more air, so that the tunnels are well ventilated.

The female lines a den with grass. This is where she will raise her family.

SEWING NESTS TO MEASURE

Tailor ants (or weaver ants) live in subtropical forests, where they build their nests in rolled-up leaves. While some of the ants hold the edges of two leaves close with their jaws and feet, others bind them together using a "thread" of silky glue produced by the ant larvae. Each larva has some glue inside it. To get it out, the adults squeeze a larva's abdomen, a bit like using a tube of glue. This doesn't harm the larvae, which continue to grow.

Prairie dogs "kiss" when they meet and groom each other. These activities help maintain a close social structure among the family groups.

■ MORE ABOUT PRAIRIE DOGS

Prairie dogs are rodents in the squirrel family. They get their name from their barklike call. Prairie dogs have short tails, small ears, and grow to about 10 inches (25 cm) long. They feed on seeds, grass, and other plants, plus some insects. Once numerous in the United States and northern Mexico, the number and range of prairie dogs have been greatly reduced. They are often hunted and poisoned because they damage crops and compete with livestock for grass. At the beginning of this century, a colony of black-tailed prairie dogs was estimated to have 400 million members!

This upward-sloping den will be useful in case of flooding.

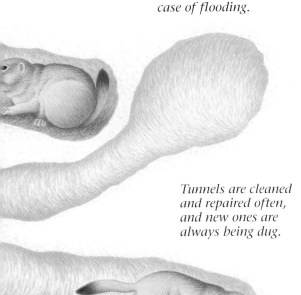

Tunnels are cleaned and repaired often, and new ones are always being dug.

CARRYING A HOME ON ITS BACK

The nautilus is a mollusk that lives in the Indian and South Pacific oceans. Its house is a many-chambered, mother-of-pearl shell about 10 inches (25 cm) in diameter. The nautilus lives in the outermost chamber. The others are all connected to the animal by tubes. The mollusk can adjust the amount of gas inside the chambers to help it float or move.

Master Builders

Many animals build solid "houses" where they can eat, rest, hide from predators, and reproduce undisturbed, even when the temperatures outside are freezing cold or sizzling hot. Some construct their homes in the water. Others build hanging nests at close quarters with hundreds of their kind, creating lively communities. Yet other species build tall and stately towers of earth with complex internal structures, including rooms and corridors large and small, where a bustling and well-organized social life exists.

A DOME IN THE WATER

Beavers build their lodges in rivers using tree trunks, branches, and shrubs, which they haul from nearby forests. They use weeds, stones, and mud as cement. About 6 feet (2 m) high, the lodge is dome-shaped with an airhole at the top. The entrance is always underwater. If the river isn't deep enough, these amazing rodents build a dam, transforming a part of the river into a small lake where they can dive and swim. The dam isolates and protects the lodge.

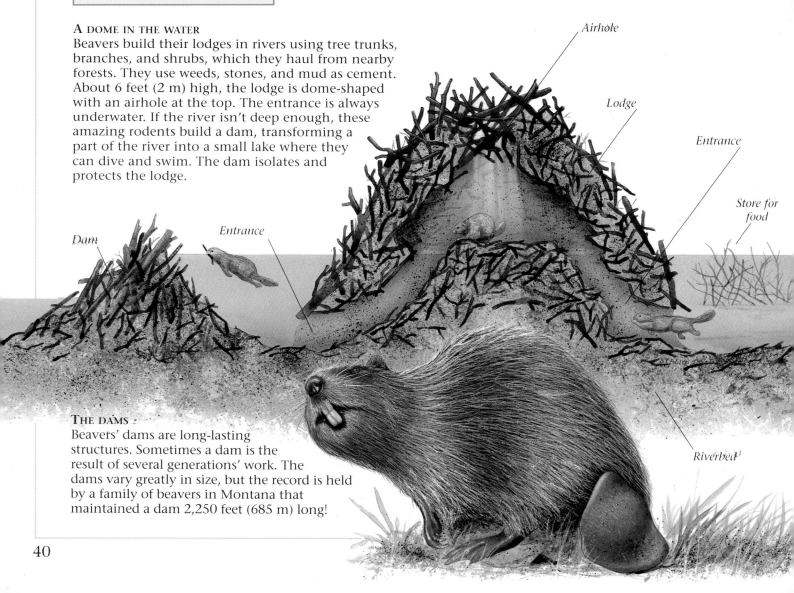

Airhole

Lodge

Entrance

Store for food

Dam

Entrance

Riverbed

THE DAMS

Beavers' dams are long-lasting structures. Sometimes a dam is the result of several generations' work. The dams vary greatly in size, but the record is held by a family of beavers in Montana that maintained a dam 2,250 feet (685 m) long!

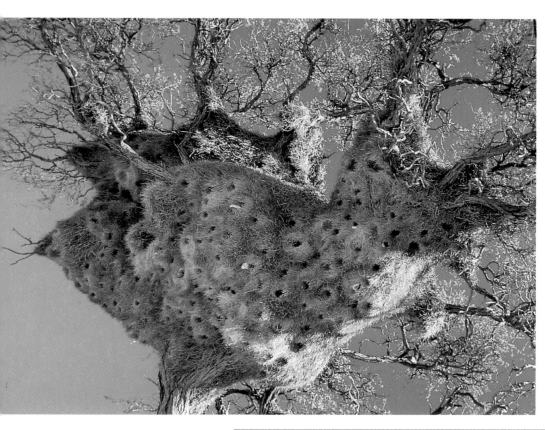

HANGING CITIES
On the savannas of southwest Africa lives a small bird with a taste for building combined with a respect for the privacy of its neighbors. Groups of weaverbirds build huge communal nests up to 16 feet (4.9 m) across. These "cities" are built nest by nest on the branches of trees or on telephone poles and may contain over 100 entrance holes. In these hanging cities, every couple has its own living space.

A PALACE FIT FOR A QUEEN
The dry grasslands of Africa also are home to termites and their tall and almost indestructible homes. Termites need a constant temperature to survive, and their mounds are designed to regulate both heat and humidity. A complex network of chambers and corridors creates a well-ventilated environment. In termite society, roles are assigned at birth. The queen termite spends her life laying eggs, while millions of worker termites bring food and clean and maintain the "palace." There also are soldier termites who defend the termite hill from predators.

Living Together

Sharing an environment with another species can sometimes be useful to one or both of them. They may protect one another from predators, help keep each other clean, or provide food for one another. The sea anemone and the clown fish are a perfect example of this type of harmonious relationship (see picture on the next page). Sometimes relations between two species living at close quarters can be more difficult. The South American fox, for example, benefits from living in viscachas' tunnels and, in turn, helps frighten away some of the viscachas' predators. However, when the fox begins to attack viscachas' young, the relationship ends. Often just one species will benefit from a close association. In the case of the cuckoo, which deposits its eggs in another bird's nest, the host's eggs are pushed out of the nest, and the host is forced to raise the cuckoo's offspring rather than its own.

■ MORE ABOUT VISCACHAS AND SOUTH AMERICAN FOXES

Both viscachas and South American foxes live in South America. The foxes are members of the dog family. There are several species, and they live both on the plains and in forested areas. They have long, gray hair and bushy tails. Viscachas are rodents of the chinchilla family. There are two types of viscachas. They both feed on grass. The plains viscacha is considered a pest, because its burrows disturb farmland and also because it eats feed that is intended for farm animals.

AN UNEASY RELATIONSHIP

Plains viscachas live in huge underground burrows. Surprisingly, they often tolerate the presence of South American foxes living in their burrows for at least part of the year. Things go smoothly between the two species while the fox confines itself to eating rabbits and the carcasses of dead viscachas. Trouble can arise, however, when the viscachas give birth to their young and the foxes begin to prey on them. When this happens, the viscachas quickly chase the foxes from their burrows.

"LOOKS STRANGE TO ME!"
This is what the tiny reed warbler seems to be thinking as it looks at the cuckoo chick in its nest. Cuckoo parents don't build nests but instead lay their eggs in other birds' nests. Then they fly away and leave the nest owner to raise their offspring. The cuckoo chick often throws the other eggs or chicks out of the nest so that it will get all the foster parents' care.

AN UNLIKELY FRIENDSHIP
Sea anemones are highly poisonous. They feed on fish, which they sting to death with their tentacles. The clown fish, however, lives among these tentacles, apparently immune to the stings and poison. Both species benefit from the arrangement. The clown fish is safe from predators, while the sea anemone is kept clean and safe from some of its own enemies.

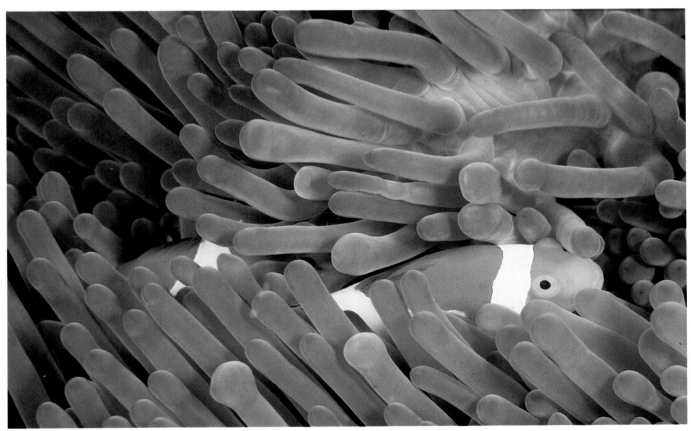

Warning Signals

Keeping safe is a full-time job for many animals. A fast escape or the subtle blending into the surrounding environment often are preceded by special warning signals. Animals that live in groups have learned that they will be safer if they take turns keeping watch. Other creatures have bright colors to warn predators that they are poisonous or taste bad. Some harmless animals frighten predators away by **mimicking** the appearance of more dangerous species.

A WHITE FLASH
While they graze, the individuals in a herd of pronghorns raise their heads frequently in order to watch for predators. As soon as danger appears, often in the form of a wolf or a human, the guard raises the white hair on its rump. At this silent signal, the whole herd flees at high speed.

A LONG NECK FOR SAFETY
The ostrich, the largest bird in the world, is easy to see, even at a distance. It lives in a continual state of alert, never sleeping for more than 15 minutes at a time. Its survival depends on its long neck and keen eyesight that allow it to spot predators from a distance. Other methods of defense include puffing up its feathers so that it looks like a bush, kicking, and, if all else fails, running away. Ostriches can reach speeds of up to 45 miles per hour (72 kph).

SPOT THE **DIFFERENCE**
What's the difference between the two snakes shown below? The one in the top photo is a coral snake, and it is deadly poisonous. The snake shown in the bottom photo is called a false coral snake. It has a nasty but nonlethal bite. The colorful pattern both snakes share warns predators to keep away.

WATCH OUT!
The dangerous-looking "snake" shown above keeps predators at a safe distance. This is how the harmless great mormon caterpillar disguises itself to frighten birds and other predators. By swelling up its rear end, which has large, eyelike markings, it resembles a small viper. To make the show even more convincing, it sways backward and forward and makes hissing noises.

"**D**ON'T BITE ME. I'M POISONOUS!"
The arrow poison frog advertises the fact that it is poisonous with its bold colors. Bright colors usually warn potential predators of bad taste, poison, or a sting. This frog has glands in its skin that release a highly toxic liquid covering its whole body. The Indians who share its forest environment use the toxin to poison the ends of their arrows. The liquid is not just a poison, but also a painkiller and an antibiotic.

After they hatch, the tadpoles of some arrow poison frog species are carried on their father's back.

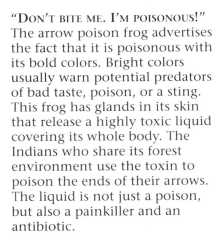

Competition

Most habitats are populated by many different plant and animal species. The problem is, sharing an environment is not always easy. Furious fights can break out when food is scarce or when the best places to build a nest or den are taken. Some animals, like snowy sheathbills, will steal food from others instead of hunting for themselves. Scavengers, such as hyenas and vultures, don't always wait until the successful hunter has finished eating. They often move in beforehand to claim the kill. At mating time, competition within a species may also occur as the males fight to win control over mating rights. In most cases, the strongest animal will win, although intelligence and skill also are important factors in overcoming competitors.

STEALING MEALS
Snowy sheathbills live around the southern shores of the world, near the South Pole. They are **opportunistic feeders** and often are found scavenging in garbage heaps around whaling stations. They breed near penguin colonies, from which they steal eggs to eat. Otherwise a mated pair will work together to rob penguin parents of **krill** before they can feed it to their youngsters. Although the penguins are upset by these attacks, there is little they can do to defend themselves from the bold snowy sheathbills.

■ **MORE ABOUT ELEPHANT SEALS**
Elephant seals are the largest members of the seal suborder. There are two types of elephant seals. The northern species lives off the coast of California and Mexico. The southern species lives in the cold sub-Antarctic regions. Elephant seals also are known as sea elephants because of their size and because of the male's inflatable trunklike snout. Males (called bulls) can grow up to 18 feet (5.5 m) long and weigh almost 8,000 pounds (3,600 kg). Elephant seals eat fish, crustaceans, and squid. They breed and **molt** on land but spend the rest of the year at sea.

RIVALS IN LOVE
At winter's end, male elephant seals head toward land, where each will try to stake out a stretch of territory and establish a **harem** of females. Since many males arrive on the same beaches, furious fighting soon breaks out. The battles continue until a champion bull has beaten all other contenders. Only then do the females come ashore. After just a few days, they give birth to pups conceived the year before. When the pups are about a month old, the adults mate again. The head bull mates with all the 15 to 30 cows in his harem.

SCAVENGING FROM SCAVENGERS
A cheetah catches a Thomson's gazelle after a brief, high-speed chase. As it tears its victim apart and begins its meal, it is surrounded by a pack of hyenas. Outnumbered, the big cat makes a hasty retreat while the hyenas move in. As they feast on the carcass, vultures circle above. When the hyenas have eaten their fill, the vultures will clean the bones of any remaining meat. In just a few hours, the body of an animal is reduced to bare bones.

Flight

Of all animals, birds, with their strong wings and light feathers, are best suited to life in the air. Their streamlined bodies are perfectly adapted for flight. Their bones, many of which are hollow, are strong and light. Birds breathe using their lungs, but they also have air sacs that extend through the body and into the hollow bones. These make the birds even lighter and also function as an air-cooling system. Some other animals, such as the flying squirrel (right) or the flying fish, also venture into the air, but they can only glide. The only other true fliers are bats and insects.

These seagulls show some of the key wing movements used in flight.

Inside a bird's wing bone

THE WING
A bird's wing is highly specialized. The internal bone structure is extremely light yet strong. Many of the bones are hollow except for a few internal struts for strength. The bones at the tips are strong and flexible, enabling birds to circle and dive with ease. When a bird flaps its wings up and down, air moving over them creates lift (pushing the bird up), while the backward push of the wings forces the bird forward.

GLIDING LEAPS

Flying squirrels are able to make gliding leaps of well over 100 feet (30 m). They have a special fold of furry skin attached on each side of their body between the front and rear leg. It spreads out like a parachute as they jump.

FORMATION FLYING

Flocks of birds on long-distance flights will often form a "V" shape. Scientists think they do this to save energy. By flying closely behind and slightly above the bird in front, each bird gets a small updraft of air. Because the front bird has to work harder than the others, after a few hours it will drop back, and another will take its place.

UP AND AWAY

There are more than 50 species of fish, mainly inhabitants of tropical seas, that are able to glide for a relatively long distance above the water's surface. They are called flying fish. With a predator hot on its tail, a flying fish builds up speed underwater and then shoots out of the ocean to make a long, gliding jump away from danger.

Speed

Being able to move at high speeds is an important adaptation for a number of animals. Running, leaping, flying, and swimming quickly enable them to catch their prey, escape predators, impress a mate, or travel long distances to avoid winter or reach an ideal breeding ground. Regardless of the environment in which they live, whether it be land, sea, or air, their ability to survive is closely linked to their capacity for speed. The animals shown here are examples of some of the fastest animals from different environments.

AN APPROPRIATE NAME
Swifts are the fastest of the smaller birds, reaching speeds of 70 miles per hour (112 kph). Migratory species have been known to travel 1,000 miles (1,610 km) in just 3 days. Swifts spend most of their lives in the air, either swooping or darting about to catch the insects on which they feed or flying and gliding over long distances during migration. Some biologists believe the common swift may not land at all except when breeding.

SPEEDING LAND BIRDS
Large, flightless birds, including the ostrich, cassowary, emu, and rhea, are all fast runners. Although they all have wings, these birds have lost the ability to fly and now rely on running to escape predators. Ostriches have been timed at over 45 miles per hour (72 kph).

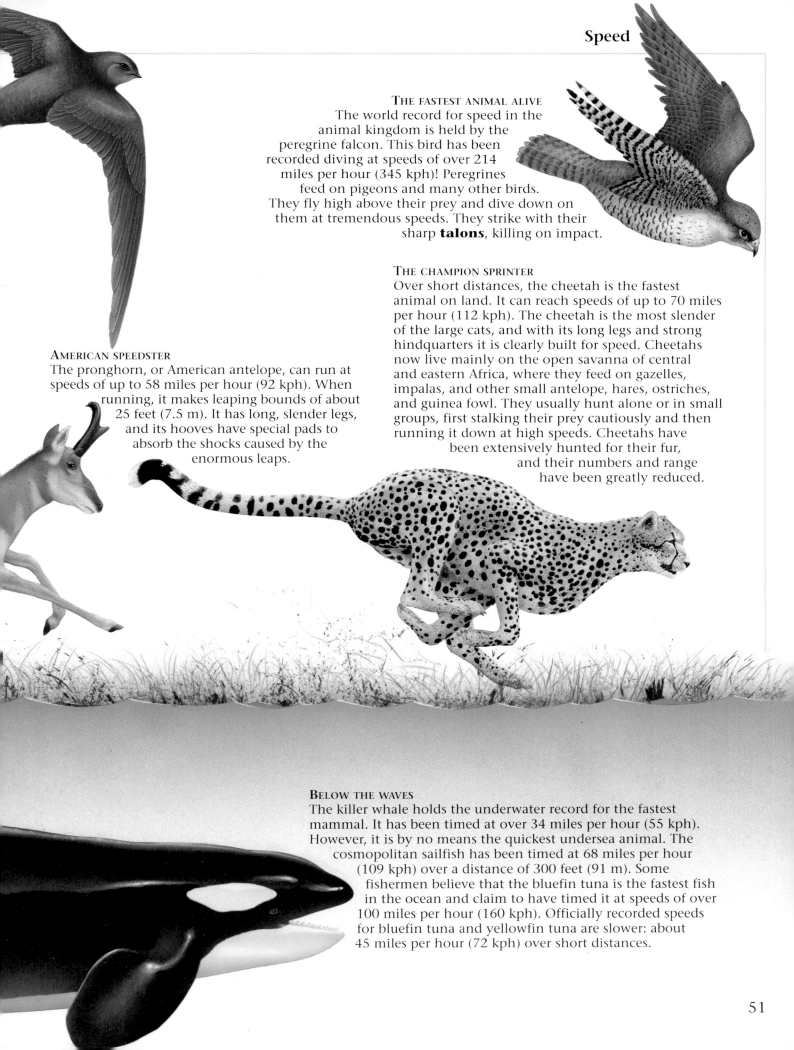

THE FASTEST ANIMAL ALIVE

The world record for speed in the animal kingdom is held by the peregrine falcon. This bird has been recorded diving at speeds of over 214 miles per hour (345 kph)! Peregrines feed on pigeons and many other birds. They fly high above their prey and dive down on them at tremendous speeds. They strike with their sharp **talons**, killing on impact.

THE CHAMPION SPRINTER

Over short distances, the cheetah is the fastest animal on land. It can reach speeds of up to 70 miles per hour (112 kph). The cheetah is the most slender of the large cats, and with its long legs and strong hindquarters it is clearly built for speed. Cheetahs now live mainly on the open savanna of central and eastern Africa, where they feed on gazelles, impalas, and other small antelope, hares, ostriches, and guinea fowl. They usually hunt alone or in small groups, first stalking their prey cautiously and then running it down at high speeds. Cheetahs have been extensively hunted for their fur, and their numbers and range have been greatly reduced.

AMERICAN SPEEDSTER

The pronghorn, or American antelope, can run at speeds of up to 58 miles per hour (92 kph). When running, it makes leaping bounds of about 25 feet (7.5 m). It has long, slender legs, and its hooves have special pads to absorb the shocks caused by the enormous leaps.

BELOW THE WAVES

The killer whale holds the underwater record for the fastest mammal. It has been timed at over 34 miles per hour (55 kph). However, it is by no means the quickest undersea animal. The cosmopolitan sailfish has been timed at 68 miles per hour (109 kph) over a distance of 300 feet (91 m). Some fishermen believe that the bluefin tuna is the fastest fish in the ocean and claim to have timed it at speeds of over 100 miles per hour (160 kph). Officially recorded speeds for bluefin tuna and yellowfin tuna are slower: about 45 miles per hour (72 kph) over short distances.

Light and Dark

Some habitats, such as caves or ocean depths, are always shrouded in complete darkness. Many animals that live in the dark have developed specialized lighting systems to aid in hunting or recognizing others of their species. Some animals in more normal environments are nocturnal, which means they are active at night. Some of them also use "body lights" to attract prey or partners or to warn off enemies. Some **diurnal** (active during the day) animals have learned to exploit daylight for hunting, feeding, or hiding.

SURVIVING IN THE DEPTHS

Deep-sea fish need special adaptations to survive the extreme pressure, continual darkness, and cold that are normal conditions of the ocean depths. Viperfish have enlarged eyes and light-producing organs along their sides to cope with the dark. The lights serve to attract other fish on which they feed. They are also used for recognizing fish of the same species during courtship. Viperfish take their name from their unusually large teeth, which look as scary as a viper's fangs.

GLEAMING WATER

Some nights the surface of the ocean gleams dully in the dark. This is not reflected moonlight but often groups of luminous jellyfish moving along just below the surface. Their gelatinous bodies glow with a weak, pinkish violet light.

MORE ABOUT VULTURES
There are about twenty species of vultures. They are divided into two groups—Old and New World vultures. The two groups are not closely related. Most vultures have bare heads and feet that are specially adapted for gripping the carcasses of dead animals as they tear them apart. Most vultures don't hunt live prey but instead prefer to eat carrion (the flesh of dead animals).

KEEN EYES
As the turkey vulture soars high in the sky, it tilts its head from side to side so that its keen eyes can focus on the ground. When it spots a meal—a dead deer, for example—it swoops down to tear at the flesh with its hooked beak. Other vultures soon join in the feast.

A female glowworm (a wingless firefly), glowing to attract a male during courtship.

INSECT CODES
Fireflies are nocturnal beetles that live in tropical, subtropical, and temperate regions throughout the world. They have special light-producing organs on the underside of their abdomen, which they use to signal other fireflies during courtship. Each species has its own pattern of long and/or short flashes, which males and females use to recognize each other. Some biologists think the flashes are also used for defense, reminding predators that fireflies have a bitter taste.

Resting

Nearly all animals spend at least part of the day or night sleeping. The amount of rest each species needs varies greatly. For example, in a 24-hour period, sloths and bats sleep for about 20 hours, chimpanzees and rabbits need about 10 hours' rest, while elephants spend only 3 hours sleeping. Biologists don't really know why animals need different amounts of rest, just as they don't completely understand the function of sleep in any animal, including humans. The most vulnerable animals, such as antelope, tend to sleep less. Animals that need to eat continually also spend very little time resting. Some animals take long periods of rest, usually in the winter, called hibernation.

■ **MORE ABOUT SHARKS**
There are over 200 species of sharks. They live in oceans throughout the world. Despite their vicious reputation, most sharks are harmless to humans. A few species feed on plankton, while most feed on other fish, including smaller sharks, squid, and shellfish. The great white shark is one of the few that does sometimes attack people, but the frequency with which they strike is exaggerated. Unlike other fish, most sharks give birth to live young rather than laying eggs.

SLEEPY SHARKS
Until recently, it was thought that sharks never slept. But when divers began to go below the surface at night, aided by flashlights, they were surprised to find that these creatures do indeed go to sleep. They rest in underwater caves and crevices, one beside the other, in large groups. They usually sleep when their stomachs are full.

Nurse sharks slumbering in an underwater cave

CAUGHT NAPPING

Most birds cannot see well enough at night to fly. At dusk they head for special roosting places where they spend the night. Many birds also take short naps during the day. Wading birds, like this flamingo, rest standing in the water on one foot with their heads tucked into their wings. Although they are sleeping, they keep one eye open and are able to spot any approaching danger. Even so, once they get into their napping position, they are reluctant to put their foot down and will hop out of the way of all but the most threatening dangers.

THE LONGEST SLEEP

Some animals rest when the weather is too cold, too hot, or too dry, when sources of food are scarce, or when they are most vulnerable to predators. When conditions are favorable, they eat enough food to build up reserves of body fat. Then they settle down in a nest or burrow and sleep until the weather and availability of food improves again. This long period of rest is called hibernation. Animals that commonly hibernate in the winter include squirrels, hedgehogs, marmots, and bats. Rodents, including dormice, are the only animals that store food in their winter nests. After several weeks, they wake up, have a snack, then settle down again for another few weeks' slumber.

SLEEPING ON THE WING

Many species of birds make long migratory journeys, sometimes traveling hundreds or even thousands of miles each year. As the birds travel, they need to rest, but instead of interrupting their journey, they often sleep as they fly. These greylags, or common wild geese, live in many parts of the Northern Hemisphere.

Blending In

How do animals avoid predators they would rather not meet face-to-face? Some flee, others hide or play dead, others still simply make themselves almost invisible by imitating the shapes and colors of the surrounding environment. This explains why we sometimes see twigs that move, yellowing leaves that jump, or eyes blinking in a snowy landscape. Some animals, including the ptarmigan, change their appearance with the seasons. The chameleon and some fish can change color within minutes to match different backgrounds.

SEA HORSE, OR SEAWEED?
A very special sea horse, called the leafy sea dragon, lives among the kelp beds off the eastern coast of Australia. Its body has gradually taken on the form and transparency of seaweed, so that it is practically indistinguishable from the real thing and thus safer from predators.

A TWIG THAT MOVES

Sitting perfectly still in the bushes, the walkingstick is almost identical to a twig and therefore safer from predators. This greenish brown night feeder, which sometimes grows to a length of 12 inches (30 cm), sleeps during the day clinging to a stem the same color as its body.

A COAT FOR EVERY SEASON

In the snow-covered landscape of the freezing Arctic winter, only the movement of its dark eyes betrays the presence of the white-tailed ptarmigan. The eagles, snowy owls, and ermines that hunt it have difficulty picking out its form against the white background. Come spring, it begins to molt and is a speckled brownish white, just like the landscape. In the summer, its coat is brown, yellow, black, and white, to match the surrounding vegetation.

LONG-LASTING COLOR CHANGE

Before the industrial revolution, a peppered moth sitting on the lichen-covered branch of a birch tree was very difficult to see. Then, as factories began to pour out smoke, the lichen died, and the bark turned black. These moths, once a symbol of the open countryside and clean air, became easy prey for birds. But halfway through the last century, a darker peppered moth developed, which safely blended with the bark. Recently, with tough antipollution laws, factories produce less smoke. Now both the trees and the moths are lightening in color again.

Finding the Way

Many animals make long journeys, sometimes traveling thousands of miles in search of warmer climates, more abundant food, or to reproduce where they themselves were born. Scientists don't fully understand how the animals know which way to go. Many explanations have been offered, including instinct, following an older member of a group, navigating by the stars, using ultrasound to create mental "maps," or being sensitive to and then following the Earth's magnetic field. None of these theories is completely satisfactory. Other animals have highly specialized senses and techniques for hunting and finding their way.

A TROPICAL JOURNEY
Common freshwater eels live in rivers and streams throughout the world. When it is time to breed, they move to saltwater. The eels of Europe and North America make long journeys to the Sargasso Sea, off the coast of Florida. For European eels, this means crossing the Atlantic Ocean, a distance of some 4,000 miles (6,430 km). The slow-moving, warm waters of the Sargasso are ideal for eel larvae. The tiny larvae drift into the Gulf Stream and begin their journey back to their parents' homeland. European larvae take three years to get back to Europe. When they reach the coasts, they change into miniature eels, called elvers. They swim up rivers where they live for five to eight years before making the long journey again.

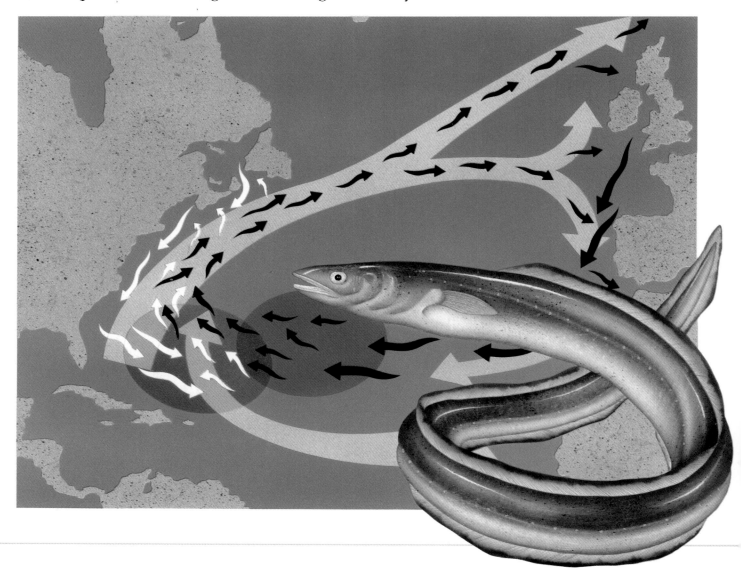

Sensitive beaks

The Australian platypus is a unique creature. It has been described as having the fur of a mole, the tail of a beaver, and the webbed feet of a frog. Although mammals, platypus mothers lay eggs. Scientists have also discovered that platypuses hunt underwater with their eyes, ears, and noses tightly shut. They find their favorite foods (worms, insect larvae, freshwater shrimp, small fish, and frogs) by means of the electro- and touch-receptors that line their leathery beaks.

Hunting by radar

Bats hunt at night. Most use a sophisticated system called **echolocation** to track down their prey. They send out a series of high-pitched screeches at regular intervals and then listen for the echoes that bounce off an insect's body. By listening to the echoes, they can tell where an insect is and at what distance. Echolocation allows bats to hunt in complete darkness. The shrieks are too high-pitched for the human ear to hear, but insects recognize the sound from a distance and try to avoid their predators.

Glossary

Adaptation Evolutionary change in a plant or animal that increases its ability to survive and reproduce in its environment.

Blubber Thick, insulating layer of fat under the skin of aquatic mammals, such as whales.

Canopy Second highest layer of a tropical rain forest. The leaves and branches of the trees grow so close to each other that almost no sunlight reaches lower levels. Only emergents grow above the canopy.

Carnivore Any meat-eating animal. More specifically any member of the mammalian order Carnivora, which includes cats, bears, dogs, and badgers.

Colony Group of animals that live close together.

Current Mass of air or water that has a steady flow in a particular direction.

Deciduous Trees that shed their leaves each year at the end of the growing season, usually in the fall.

Diurnal An animal that is active during daylight hours.

Domestic Any animal bred or tamed by people for work, for food, or as a household pet.

Dormant State in which a plant or animal reduces or suspends activity, usually because of unfavorable conditions.

Echolocation Finding the position of an object by measuring the time taken for an echo to return from it.

Emergent Plant that sticks out above the top of the tall canopy of trees in a rain forest.

Endangered species Plant or animal species that is in danger of extinction (dying out). It is usually as a result of human activities, such as the destruction of natural habitats, pollution, and hunting.

Environment Surroundings in which a plant or animal lives, and which influence its development and behavior.

Evergreen Tree that retains its foliage throughout the year.

Evolution Process by which plants and animals change over successive generations. The result is often better adaptation to the environment and eventually production of new species.

Extinction Death of the last remaining individuals of a species of plant or animal. This may be caused by predators or by changes in climate or habitat.

Food chain Series of organisms, each one of which is a food source for another. A simple chain might start with grass, which is eaten by rabbits, which are then eaten by foxes or hawks. The remains of dead plants and animals may be eaten by scavengers or be broken down by bacteria.

Gland Organ in an animal's body that secretes useful chemical substances, such as hormones and digestive juices.

Habitat An animal's or a plant's natural surroundings, such as forest, freshwater, or the seashore.

Harem Permanent or temporary group of animals, consisting of one breeding male and several females, each with her own young.

Herbivore An animal that feeds on plants.

Hibernation Period of winter sleep, during which an animal's metabolism (bodily functions) slows down, and its temperature drops as low as that of the environment.

Incubation 1. Keeping eggs safe or warm until they hatch. 2. Period of time between laying and hatching of an egg.

Invertebrate Any animal without a backbone.

Jurassic Period Geological period between 135 and 200 million years ago when dinosaurs and other reptiles flourished.

Krill Tiny shrimplike crustaceans that live in huge swarms in the oceans. They are an important food source for baleen whales and other sea creatures.

Larva (plural larvae) Stage in the metamorphosis of certain animals, such as butterflies and frogs. Caterpillars and tadpoles are larvae.

Lichens Unusual organisms that consist of an intricate mixture of a fungus and an alga. Slow-growing and hardy, they can survive on rocks, tree trunks, and walls. In the tundra they are an important source of food for grazing animals.

Mammal Any member of the class Mammalia. All have at least some hair. Most give birth to active, live young. The female feeds her young on milk from her body. Humans, monkeys, cats, mice, and whales are all mammals.

Microscopic Too small to be seen without the aid of a microscope.

Migration Regular movement of animals from one area to another and back again at certain times of the year.

Mimicry When an animal, usually harmless, resembles another, usually harmful, animal and thereby gains protection from predators who fear to attack it.

Mollusk Any member of the phylum Mollusca; the name means soft, and most mollusks are soft-bodied, though many have shells.

Molt To shed feathers, hair, or skin.

Muzzle Projecting part of an animal's head, including its nose and mouth.

Nocturnal Animals that are active during the night.

Omnivore Any animal that feeds on both plants and other animals. Most humans are omnivores.

Opportunistic feeder Animal that will eat whatever food it can find, by hunting, scavenging, or stealing food from others.

Pack ice Large masses of ice floating on the ocean, resulting from the breakup of sea ice in the spring.

Permafrost Permanently frozen subsoil in the polar regions.

Plankton Masses of minute plants and animals that float on or just beneath the surface of lakes, rivers, and oceans. They provide valuable food for larger animals.

Predator Any carnivorous animal that hunts and kills other animals (prey).

Regurgitate To bring swallowed, partially digested food up again to the mouth.

Reptile Any member of the class Reptilia; vertebrates with scaly skin. They include snakes and lizards.

Rodents Large group of mammals that includes rats, mice, beavers, and squirrels. Their strong incisors (front teeth) grow continuously but are worn down by gnawing.

Roe rings Tracks left by male roe deer during courtship in late summer.

Savanna Name given to the vast grassy plains of tropical Africa where there are few or no trees.

Scavenger An animal that feeds on dead bodies and other decaying matter. They play an important role clearing away food and droppings left by other animals.

Selective breeding Selection and pairing of plants or animals to improve the quality of their offspring. Only the best, most useful individuals are allowed to become parents.

Snow line Level on a mountain or in the polar regions beyond which snow never entirely melts.

Spawn 1. Eggs of fish or frogs. 2. To lay large numbers of eggs in water.

Subsoil Broken-up rock below the surface soil.

Talons Elongated, hooked claws of birds of prey.

Territory Area inhabited and defended by an animal or group of animals against others of the same species.

Ultrasonic Sound waves or vibrations with a frequency that cannot be heard by the human ear.

Index

Further Reading

Cherfas, Jeremy. *Animal Defenses*. Lerner, 1991.
Landau, Elaine. *Mountain Mammals*. Childrens, 1996.
Massa, Renato and Monica Carabella. *Coniferous Forest*. Raintree Steck-Vaughn, 1997.
Savage, Stephen. *Animals of the Desert*. Raintree Steck-Vaughn, 1997.
_____. *Animals of the Grasslands*. Raintree Steck-Vaughn, 1997.

Acknowledgments

The Publishers would like to thank the following photographers and archives for permission to reproduce pictures and for their assistance in providing pictures. The sources of the photographs are listed below. The following short forms have been used:

CAPPELLI = Giuliano Cappelli, Florence
CERFOLLI = Fulvio Cerfolli, Rome
JACANA = Jacana, Paris
NARDI = Marco Nardi, Florence
OKAPIA = Okapia, Frankfurt
OSF = Oxford Scientific Films, London
OVERSEAS = Overseas, Milan
PANDA = Panda Photo, Rome

1 A. Nardi/PANDA; 4 CAPPELLI; 5 CAPPELLI; 6T Z. Leszczynski/OVERSEAS; 6B F. Pölking/OVERSEAS; 7T CAPPELLI; 7C C. Bagnoli/PANDA; 7B CERFOLLI; 8T D. Allan/OSF–OVERSEAS; 8B C. Guinet/PANDA; 9 B. Curtsinger/OVERSEAS; 10T Dragesco/OVERSEAS; 10B CAPPELLI; 11 N. Rosing/OVERSEAS; 12T CAPPELLI; 12B L. Accusani/PANDA; 13T CAPPELLI; 13B CAPPELLI; 14T CAPPELLI; 14B G. D'Acunto/PANDA; 15 W. Shattil-B. Rozinski/OSF–OVERSEAS; 14T CAPPELLI; 16T CAPPELLI; 16B CAPPELLI; 17 CAPPELLI; 18 Varin-Visage/JACANA–OVERSEAS; 19TL/19TR M. Fogden/OSF–OVERSEAS; 20T M. Fogden/OSF–OVERSEAS; 20B J. A. L. Cooke/OSF–OVERSEAS; 21 M. Wendler/OVERSEAS; 22T CAPPELLI; 22C FLPA/PANDA; 22B E. Dragesco/PANDA; 23 CAPPELLI; 24T M. Andera/PANDA; 24B CAPPELLI; 25T D. Thompson/OSF–OVERSEAS; 25C J. A. L. Cooke/OSF–OVERSEAS; 26T L. Vinco/PANDA; 26B CERFOLLI; 27C M. Lanfranchi/OVERSEAS; 27B CERFOLLI; 29T C. Monteath/OVERSEAS; 29C GREENPEACE/OVERSEAS; 29B J. D. Watt/PANDA; 30 H. Hall/OSF–OVERSEAS; 31 C. Dani-I. Jeske/OVERSEAS; 32T Klein-Hubert/PANDA; 32B CAPPELLI; 33T NARDI; 33C H. Ausloos/PANDA; 34T N. Bromhall/OSF–OVERSEAS; 34B L. Crowhurst/OSF–OVERSEAS; 35 G. Saltini–M. Mattoccia/PANDA; 36T G. Marcoaldi/PANDA; 36C X. Eichaker/PANDA; 36B Varin/JACANA–OVERSEAS; 36R K. Aitken/PANDA; 37L CAPPELLI; 38 CAPPELLI; 39T J. A. L. Cooke/OSF–OVERSEAS; 39B R. Kuiter/OSF–OVERSEAS; 41T M. Brooke/OSF–OVERSEAS; 41B Hervy/JACANA–OVERSEAS; 43T CAPPELLI; 43B D. Fleetham/OSF–OVERSEAS; 44 CAPPELLI; 45TL Varin/JACANA–OVERSEAS; 45TR B. Tognon/PANDA; 45C C. Bagnoli/PANDA; 45B M. Fogsen/OSF–OVERSEAS; 47T D. Allan/OSF–OVERSEAS; 47B CAPPELLI; 48T R. A. Wood/OVERSEAS; 48C CERFOLLI; 49T CAPPELLI; 49B Pilloud/JACANA–OVERSEAS; 52T Russotti/OVERSEAS; 52B P. Parkes/OSF–OVERSEAS; 53C A. Compost/PANDA; 53B R. Blythe/OSF–OVERSEAS 55T CAPPELLI; 55C O. Newman/OSF–OVERSEAS; 55B CAPPELLI; 56T CAPPELLI; 56B A. H. Kuiter/OSF–OVERSEAS; 57TR CAPPELLI; 57TL P. Parks/OSF–OVERSEAS; 57C Varin-Visage/JACANA–OVERSEAS; 57BR CAPPELLI; 59T A. Root/OKAPIA–OVERSEAS; 59B S. Dalton/OSF–OVERSEAS